Seed-Babies

An Illustrated Children's Story of Plants, Eggs and Seeds in Nature

By Margaret Warner Morley

Published by Pantianos Classics

ISBN-13: 978-1-78987-170-8

First published in 1898

Contents

It will add very much to their interest in seeds if the children have peas, beans, nuts, etc., to look at as they read about them.

Seed-Babies

Beans

I.

"**W**ell, I never!"

Jack said that because all the beans he had planted were on top of the ground.

Jack was only six years old, and not very well acquainted with beans.

No wonder he was surprised to find them on top of the ground when he had tucked them so snugly out of sight in the brown earth only a few days before.

Jack looked at his beans and began to get red in the face.

He looked a little as if he were going to cry.

"When Ko comes I'll just punch him!" he said at last.

For who could have uncovered his beans but his brother Ko?

For Ko would rather tease than eat his dinner, — except when there was choco-late pudding for dessert.

Ko's real name was Nicholas, but it took too long to say that, so Jack called him Ko for short.

Jack picked up a bean to replant it, and what do you think had happened?

Something had, for it did not look as it did when he first put it in the ground.

It had turned green to begin with. Jack had planted white beans.

He knew they were white all through, for he had bitten a good many in two to see how they looked inside. And now the coat on the outside, that stuck so tightly at first, had peeled half off, and the bean was green!

Something more had happened, — a little white stem had come out of the bean and gone into the ground.

Jack was so surprised at all this that he forgot he was angry at Ko, and when his brother came up only told him to look.

Ko tried to pick up a bean too, but it was fastened quite firmly in the ground.

"They're. growing," said Ko.

"Did you pull them up?" asked Jack.

"No, indeed!" said Ko.

"They must have pulled themselves up," said Jack.

6

"Yes," said Ko, "that's it. They grew so fast they pulled themselves right up."

Then Jack sprinkled earth over them until he could not see them, and went away.

In two or three days they were all on top of the ground again!

"Well, well, well!" said Jack, "they don't know anything — to keep unplanting themselves that way!"

But now he could not pick up any of the beans without tearing loose the stout little stem with roots at the end, that had gone down into the ground.

"You bean," he said, tapping one on its green head, — for they had grown very green now, — "you bean, I shall plant you deep enough this time; you will die and not grow at all if you don't stay still in the ground."

At this the bean smiled.

A bean cannot smile, you say? Oh, well, that is what nearly everybody would say, but I can tell you, a great many people do not know about beans, and I am sure that bean smiled.

"If I did stay still in the ground, how could I grow?" asked the bean. You think beans can-not talk? Well, as I said before, a great many people do not know about beans; and whether they can talk or not, this bean I asked Jack how it could grow if it stayed still in the ground. And what is more. Jack was "stumped," as the boys say, by the question, and could not answer.

7

Of course nothing that stayed perfectly still could grow.

"But why don't you send up a little stem and let the bean that I planted stay planted?" asked Jack.

"I will tell you," said the bean; and if by this time you do not believe beans can talk, you may as well not read another word of this story.

Talking beans are just as true as "Cinderella," or "Hop-o-my-thumb," or "Little Red Riding-Hood, or "Jack the Giant Killer," and those people.

Of course everybody knows how true *they* are.

So Jack's bean said, "I will tell you," and then asked, "Are your hands clean?"

"They're fair to middling," said Jack, looking at his hands, and for the first time in his life wishing he had washed them.

"Oh well," said the bean, "if they are not sticky it won't matter. I am going to let you look at me, but I don't want you to pull me apart, either on purpose or by accident."

"I won't," said Jack.

"Well, then, *very* gently open this green part that you planted when it was white, and that won't stay under the ground, and look."

Jack did so.

He found the green part was split in two halves, and right between the halves, fastened at the end where the root went down, were stowed away two pretty green leaves.

"My!" said Jack. "

"Well, I guess so!" said the bean, rather proudly. "You see I have these little leaves packed away even when I am white.

"But then they are also white and very, very small.

"You very likely would not even see them, at least not with your own eyes.

"You would see something if you knew where to look, but you would not see two leaves without the help of a magnifying glass.

"But I know they are there all the time."

II.

"Tell me more," said Jack. He thought it the jolliest thing in the world, as it certainly was, to have the beans talk to him.

The bean was as pleased as he was, for it liked to talk, and it could not always find so good a listener.

So it said, "I keep my two white little leaves very closely packed away between my two big hard white cotyle-dons."

9

"Your two big hard white what?" asked Jack. "Cotyledons." "My!" said Jack.

"Yes, cotyledons. You probably did not know there were two; you thought it was just one mass of white stuff. Probably you did not know my cotyledons had a coat, either."

"Yes," said Jack, "I knew that. It tears open when you grow. And I knew you split in two, on-ly I didn't know you called yourself cotyledons."

"*We* don't," said the bean, with a funny little laugh, "but it is no matter what we call our-selves, — grown-up men call our seed-leaves cotyledons."

"I would rather know what *you* call them," said Jack. "Oh, I can't tell you that; nobody can. But why don't you ask me what I mean by my seed-leaves?"

"I think you mean the two halves that come apart with the two little leaves between them," said Jack.

"Yes, so I do; but there are more than two leaves between; there is a little end that grows down and makes the root." "Yes," said Jack, "I know."

"Hush!" said the bean, "you don't know anything about it. You mustn't tell me you know. You must just keep on asking me about myself." "You are cross," said Jack. "I am not," said the bean, "I am only right." "Well, what shall I ask?" demanded Jack.

"Stupid! if you have nothing to ask, I have nothing to tell you, so good-by."

"Oh, don't," begged Jack. "I will ask and ask and ask, only don't stop telling."

"Well, ask away," said the bean. "What makes you turn green? What makes you so hard before you're planted? How do you know when it's time to wake up? Where do -"

"Just hear the boy!" interrupted the bean, "asking a dozen questions and not waiting for an answer to any of them! Why don't you stop to take breath?"

"Why," said Jack, "now you can answer a long time."

"There's something in that," returned the bean, "and I will tell you about turning green. You turn green —"

"I don't," said Jack.

"Don't interrupt. I turn green because I cannot digest my food unless I do, and how am I to live without food? Even you could not live if you could not digest your food."

"I'm glad I don't turn green when I digest my food," said Jack; then asked, "What do you eat?"

"There you go again, "another question and the first set not answered yet. I get my food from the air and the earth. I am fond of gas, and when I turn green I can digest it. You know the air is nothing but gas. Well, I can eat air."

11

"I'm glad I don't have to," said Jack, thinking of choco-late pudding.

"Oh, of course, you prefer much coarser things, but don't inter-rupt. I am fond of air,

and the little leaves that I have stowed away need much food, so I just grow up to the top of the ground where there is to be found air and sunlight, and then I let my two little leaves draw all the good out of my cotyledons.

"They have air, too, and water, and the root sends them food, but they eat all the good out of my cotyledons as well, and that is why they grow so fast.

Look there! see that bean plant over there!

"The cotyledons are all with-ered and look like dried leaves; that is what they are, just dried leaves.

"That is the way mine will look some day.

"But I don't care, for more leaves will grow above the first two, and I shall have plenty of stem and many leaves; and after a while beautiful flowers will come, and then lots of new seeds will grow from, my flowers. You see how it is, don't you? I am just the bean baby."

"You are a great talker for a baby," said Jack.

"Oh, yes, you can't understand that, of course, but as I said before, some people do not know about beans." "You say that pretty often," said Jack.

But the bean only laughed and replied, "Well, it's true, whether you like it or not."

III.

"Can you tell me about peas?" Jack asked the bean next day. "I planted some and they stayed in the ground."

"Perhaps I can," the bean replied, "but they are different from us, and I have told you enough."

"Well, I suppose after what you have told me, I can find out something about peas for myself," said Jack.

"Of course you can," replied the bean.

"Some people never know anything, because they cannot find out without being told."

"Good-by," said Jack politely, "I am very much obliged to you"; but the bean was not so polite as Jack, for it did not answer at all.

Perhaps, however, that is the polite way among beans.

Jack was still thinking about beans when he went into the house and saw a pan of dried Lima beans soaking for dinner.

He took one up and slipped it out of its white jacket, and it fell apart in his hand, so that he saw quite plainly the little plant packed away at one end.

"It must like water better than I do — to swell itself that full," said he to himself, for the soaked beans were about twice as large as the dried ones.

"Couldn't grow a bit without it," said Jack's bean in a cross voice, popping from between his fingers back into the pan of water, "we have begun to grow, we have."

In spite of its crossness Jack felt a little sorry that it was to be eaten for dinner instead of growing in some damp and lovely place, "but," he thought, and no doubt he was right, "maybe among beans it doesn't matter if they are eaten. I don't know beans," he added, screwing up one eye.

"Why do we eat beans?" he asked his father at dinner.

"Because they are nearly all starch, and starch is good food," his father replied.

"Does the baby bean eat starch?" Jack asked. "Oh, yes," his father said, "the baby bean grows on the starch stored up in the bean. The little plant is stowed away in one corner of the bean, and lives on the starch of the cotyledons when it first begins to grow."

"Yes, I know," said Jack, "but don't you think it is rather hard on the bean for us to eat it?"

"No," his father replied, "there would not be room for all the beans to grow. Some would have to die anyway; and if the beau could understand, I am sure it would be very glad to give us food."

"Perhaps it *does* understand," said Jack thoughtfully. "Beans are great thinkers."

"If that is so," said papa, smiling, "they must be a little proud to know that all the animals depend upon the plant life for food."

"I don't see how that is," said Ko. "Well, I will tell you," said his father. "Plants can eat gases and other minerals."

"Yes, I know that," said Jack, remembering what the bean had told him about it.

"They change these things into plant material," his father went on, "and people, who cannot eat earth and air, eat the plants, and so all are able to live."

"But we might live on meat," said Jack.

"But what makes meat?" asked his father. "What do the animals we use for meat live on?"

"Plants," Jack replied, nodding his head to show he understood.

"Yes, plants; and so, first or last, all the animals depend upon the plants for their lives."

"If we keep on we shall know beans," Ko said to Jack in a very sleepy tone of voice that night. But Jack, tucked up in his crib, was already in the Land of Nod.

Sweet Peas

"You don't seem to have to come out of the ground to get started," Jack said to his sweet peas one day.

"Oh, no," was the reply.

"But why? Don't you need air and light?'

"Yes; but we have enough food stored underground to start us, and, as a matter of fact, we prefer to lie still and let our clean, fresh leaves go out into the world."

"Do garden peas act the same way as sweet peas? asked Jack, very much awake by this time to what was going on in the garden.

"Yes," the sweet pea said, in a voice as musical as a summer brook. "Yes, the garden peas are our cousins, - our country cousins, as it were; they grow in the same way we do, and we are very fond of them."

"Do you have a baby in your seed, too? Demanded Jack, sitting down cross-legged on the ground to have a good, comfortable chat with his new friends.

"My seed *is* a baby pea," was the reply. "Between my two round cotyledons you can see the rest of the infant tucked away, ready when warmth and moisture come, to spring up and grow into a vine.

"Yes, that's so," Jack said, slowly; then added, "Ain't you afraid to stay out in the garden all night?" It had come over him all of a sudden that *he* would be very much afraid.

"Do you mean, '*Aren't* you afraid'?" asked the pea, politely but a little severely.

"Ye-e-s," said Jack, half a mind to rebel against having to correct bad grammar out of school, but not wanting to offend the pea either; "Aren't you afraid?"

"No, I am not afraid. We plants love the night-time. We can see as well as in the day-time."

Jack wanted to ask if they could see at any time without eyes, but feared it might be considered impolite.

The pea replied to his thought. "Not as you see, but we have a way of knowing about things that you see. I cannot explain how it is, for you are not a pea and could not understand."

"Can you hear?" asked Jack.

"Not as you hear. But we have a way of knowing about things that you hear. I cannot explain how it is, for you are not a pea and could not understand." "Can you smell, or taste, or feel?" persisted Jack. "Not as you smell, or taste, or feel. But we have a way of knowing about things that you smell, and taste, and feel. I cannot explain how it is, for you are not a pea and could not understand."

"I don't seem to know peas either," muttered Jack to himself.

"No, you don't know about peas. If you did, you would know more than the President of the United States and the Principal of your school put together."

"My!" said Jack, "You will never will know all about peas," the pea went on. "You can know a good many things about them, as well as about other things, that will

17

be good for you, if you keep your eyes open and your brain working."

"How they all like to teach a feller," thought Jack, as the pea settled down as though through talking.

"Teach a, *fellow,*" said the pea, rousing up; "teach a *boy* would sound better yet."

"Teach a boy," corrected Jack meekly, and then walked off. and found Ko, and told him all the pea had said.

"You dreamed it, you silly," said Ko, with a very fine air, for he was two years older than Jack, and sometimes liked to remind his brother of this fact. "You dreamed it, and anyway 't ain't polite to listen to what people *think.*"

"No," said Jack, politely but a little severely, just as the pea had said it to him, "it *isn't* polite, but then that may be polite among peas, — you don't know peas, you must re- member that."

Peanuts

"Tell you what," said Ko, "there's a baby in this peanut."

Jack looked, and sure enough, flattened down in one corner of the peanut for safe keeping, and looking very much like the bean baby, was a young peanut baby.

"Let's plant it," said Jack.

"It's been roasted," said Ko, "you don't suppose a roasted baby would grow, do you?"

"No," said Jack, "I'm afraid it wouldn't; let's ask father."

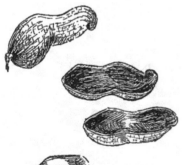

"Father says to plant it and see," Jack said, running back a few minutes later. "He says he'll get us some raw ones in town to-morrow, and we can plant both kinds."

"Of course it would be silly to plant a roasted one," said Ko.

"Why would it?" asked the peanut in his hand.

"Oh, because — it would," was the wise reply. "You're dead, you know," said Jack, "and dead things can't grow."

"Am I dead? Then how can I talk?"

19

"It *is* talking," said Ko, very much surprised as soon as he stopped to think about it.

"Anything can ask questions, whether it is dead or alive," said Jack, and a very wise speech it was, though you, who do not know as much as you will if you live to be wiser, may not think so.

"Why can't I grow?" repeated the roasted peanut.

"Well, can you?" asked Ko.

"No, I can't. Now answer my question. Why can't I?"

"I don't know," said Ko, meekly. "It's time you found that out," said the peanut, snappishly. "It is so easy for you to say a thing is so or isn't so, and all the time you don't know *anything* about it."

"I hope you 're cross enough," said Ko, firing up.

But Jack said, "Never mind, Ko, the poor thing has been roasted; if *you* had been roasted so you couldn't ever grow, you might be cross, too."

"Me, roasted! I'm not a peanut," said Ko, indignantly.

"If you knew as much as you never will know, you would understand that there is not such a great differ-ence between us as you think," said the peanut grimly; "and as to being roasted, that is by no means the worst thing that could happen in the world."

"What would be worse," asked Jack, curiously.

"I cannot tell you, you would not understand," said the peanut.

"They all seem to think alike about our understanding," said Jack.

"Yes," said Ko, "they think they know everything."

Melons and Their Cousins

"Where did you get it?" Jack asked, as he went into the yard and found Ko with a slice of ripe watermelon in his hand.

"Mother gave it to me; there's one for you," he said, pointing to another slice on a plate in the grass.

"Save the seeds," said Ko. Then for a few minutes nothing was to be heard but a funny little *juicy* sound, and when this ceased, what do you think? There was nothing left of the watermelon but just the rind and some flat, black seeds.

Ko handed a seed to Jack.

"What shall I do with it?" asked Jack.

"Take off its jacket," said Ko, speaking as though, he thought Jack a little deaf.

So Jack took the melon seed and peeled off its tough, black coat.

"Now take off its shirt," said Ko; and Jack slipped off a delicate, silky covering. "Now look inside," ordered Ko. "See!" said Jack, as he did so. The melon seed had fallen into two parts in his hand, just like the bean, and there in one end was the baby plant lying close to the cotyledons.

"Do you suppose it would grow?" asked Jack. "Of course it would," said Ko. "How do you know I would?" asked the melon seed.

"Well, wouldn't you?" asked Ko. He was used to stopping Jack's questions this way when he could not answer them, and had not yet learned the difference between Jack and a logical vegetable.

"Yes, I would," said the melon. "Now answer my question: How do you know I would?"

"Because," said Ko, confidently, "melon seeds generally do."

"Do they? How many of those you planted came up?" Ko blushed.

"You see you don't know anything about it. If you cared to be wise, you would find out how I grow, — if you could; then you would know why I don't grow and how to help me."

"That is so," said Ko, "and some day when I have plenty of time, I mean to find it out if I can."

"Let's go to the garden now and see if we can find out anything about it," said Jack. "I know where there are some jolly big melons."

"All right," said Ko, and off they went.

But they did not stay long; the melons just lay on the ground and said not a word.

"Stupid things! Come along," said Ko.

So they went along, and the first thing Jack did was to step on a ripe cucumber.

"Ouch!" he cried, and Ko laughed.

Then Jack said, "Let's make boats."

Of course I am not going to tell you what they did then, because *everybody* knows they just took cucumbers, and cut them open lengthwise, and scraped out the insides, and whittled out sticks, and stuck them in for masts, and pinned on paper sails.

They sailed their boats on the duck pond, and most of them turned over, and some sank. For the wind blew,  and Ko said there was a gale on.

If you think it is easy to make cucumber boats sail in a high wind, or in any wind, or in no wind, you just try it.

Cucumber boats do not like to sail.

Jack put a lot of seeds in his pocket; they were rather damp and sticky, but then a boy's pocket expects such things.

When the whole fleet had come to grief, the boys sat on the edge of the pond, and Jack pulled a handful of seeds out of his pocket.

"Do you suppose these are seed-babies?" he asked, holding one in his fingers.

"Easy enough to find out," said Ko, splitting one open with his finger-nail. "Yes, there it is, — a cucumber baby tucked up in the corner."

"Do you suppose *all* seeds are babies?" asked Jack, following Ko's example and splitting one open.

"I shouldn't wonder," said Ko.

"Cucumber seeds and melon seeds are just alike, only the cucumber's are small and white," said Jack.

"We're cousins," piped up the seed.

"What makes your cousins have black seeds, then?" demanded Ko.

"Won't tell," screamed the seed, "you've spoiled me and I'm mad. Go ask the pumpkins why they have white seeds, — and maybe they will tell, but I won't."

"I'm sorry I spoiled you," said Ko.

"Oh, it doesn't *really* matter," muttered the seed. "There are so many of us, we can't *all* live, and perhaps I'd rather be spoiled by you than just dry up or rot in the ground."

"Poor thing," said Ko; then added, "but I'll tell you what we'll do, Jack, when the pumpkins get ripe."

"I know," said Jack, and of course *you* know, so I wouldn't tell you for anything, how they took a pumpkin when it got ripe, and cleaned all the insides out, and cut such a lovely new moon of a mouth, in it, with scallops for teeth.

And I won't tell how they made round holes for eyes and a wedge-shaped hole for a nose. And I *never will* tell how they put a lighted candle inside, and set it on the gate post one dark night to show their father the way in, and how the telegraph boy came instead, with a message, and was frightened almost out of his senses. He was a city boy and not used to Jack-o'-lanterns. Of course Ko and Jack made the acquaintance of the pumpkin seeds, and you know as well as I do, how they found the pumpkin baby tucked away in one corner, so I won't say a word about it.

Nuts

"What did you say about nuts for dinner?" asked Jack one day.

"I said we were going to have them," replied Ko.

"It must be almost dinnertime," said Jack; and sure enough, just then the dinner bell rang.

"There's a baby in this almond, I do believe," said Jack, as he cracked his first nut, after dinner had been eaten and the nuts passed.

"It's like a bean," said Ko.

"Beans are seeds," said Jack; "if you plant them they will grow."

"So are nuts seeds," added Ko; "if you plant *them* they'll grow."

"Then there *must* be babies in the nuts," said Jack, "for it's the little seed-babies that grow up and make big plants."

"Let 's look for them in all the nuts," said Ko; then added, "Mother, can't we take our nuts on the porch and eat them?"

"Of course you may," said Mother; so off they went, their nuts in their pockets.

26

"Now," said Ko, looking very wise, "you see these almonds grow on trees, and they have to fall a long way, and they might get bruised, so *their* coat is hard like wood."

"Do you suppose that's the reason they're so hard?" asked Jack,

"It's as good a reason as any," said Ko.

"Yes," said the almond, "that is the way too many people reason, without taking the trouble to find out the real truth about things."

"Well, why are you hard?" asked Ko.

"I won't tell you," said the almond, who, though naturally good-natured, had been made Ko's poor reasoning,

"I won't tell you, because then you would never know why I am hard."

"Wouldn't I know if you told me?" asked Ko, opening his eyes in astonishment.

"No, that's the very reason you would not know. Nobody knows from being told. If you think about it as long as you live and don't ask anybody's opinion, you may find out; it's the only way."

"We'd need more than one brain, wouldn't we, if we learned everything everybody tells us to?" asked Jack.

"No, you wouldn't," said the almond; "one brain isn't much, to be sure; but if you knew enough to use it, instead of holding it open, like a big-mouthed meal-bag with a hole in the bottom, for somebody to pour things into, you would get on very well, and be as wise as would be good for you."

"Let's not eat any more almonds," said Jack, "they are so cross to us."

"Oh, no," said Ko, "they taste good, and if we eat them fast and chew them hard, they can't scold at us."

"Yes, that's the way people do about everything," said the almond with a sigh, as it disappeared in Jack's mouth.

"Do you think it will keep on talking after I 've swallowed it?" he asked, in alarm.

"Oh, I guess not," said Ko. look here!"

He had cracked a Madeira nut, and taken the meat out whole.

"I don't see any baby there," said Jack.

"Don't be too sure about that," said Ko, carefully pulling his nut apart. "Look there, in the corner! Isn't that a baby? But it lies in crosswise, not straight like the others."

"It's so crumpled up, you can't tell much about it," said Jack.

"That's it," said the nut, "I *am* crumpled; I am not smooth and simple like your bean, but here I am, all folded up, so you have to look at my cotyledons a long time to find out how I *really* split open to grow."

"How do you?" asked Ko.

"Plant me," said the Madeira nut.

The boys planted half a dozen in the garden, and dug one up every day to see how it was getting on. They gave it plenty of water and one day, — what do you think? — the shell had split open!

"Oh, Ko," screamed Jack, "just look in the crack! How white it has got!"

They planted it again; and in a day or two, out of the crack peeped a little green sprout from the place where the two crumpled cotyledons were fastened together.

The boys were delighted, but as it would say nothing to them, they planted it again and watched the stout root go down into the ground.

"Why don't its cotyledons come out of the shell?" asked Jack of Ko one day. The nut answered:

"What's the use in taking that trouble? My cotyledons are all folded in the shell, so that it would not be easy for them to get out. Besides I am so very sweet that I might get eaten if I came out. I just stay in the shell and let my leaves and roots out; they are fastened to me, you see, and can draw out all the food they need. You see my cotyledons are changed."

"Yes, they are quite soft and greenish yellow," said Ko, pulling off a piece of the shell.

"There, there! now let me alone to grow in peace," said the nut, thinking investigations had been carried far enough.

But Jack and Ko did not let it alone; they made it tell them a great many things about itself, and the great secret of how it was folded, — not at all as it *looked* to be.

But if you want to know these things, you must go and plant some Madeira nuts for yourself, and keep them moist. If they are fresh, some will be sure to sprout, and if you are as bright as I think you are, they will tell you all that Ko's and Jack's nut told them.

More About Nuts

Of course Ko and Jack did not stop there. They asked all sorts of nuts about themselves, and came to the conclusion that every nut was a seed-baby that only needed a good chance to wake up and grow.

Only some things puzzled them a great deal.

One was the hazel nut, that did not seem to have any place to split open like the rest, and the hazel only laughed at them, and would not  tell them how it got out of its shell. They thought it must be a baby, for when they cracked it, there were the two little leaves and the tiny stump of a root ready to grow, just like the other seed-babies, and of course if it were a baby it would have to get out of its shelly cradle some time, but it would not tell how.

Nor am I going to tell any tales out of school, nor in school either.

If you want to know, you will have to do as Jack and Ko did, — plant it and keep it moist.

I can tell you this much, — Jack and his brother were considerably older as well as wiser before they finally discovered the hazel nut's secret. But they did not give up until they *had* discovered it, which I hope is exactly the way you will behave.

Another thing that puzzled the boys was the Brazil nut.

They puzzled over that a long time. They couldn't make up their minds that it was a seed-baby at all; but if not, what was it?

They planted it, and one day when they were considerably older and wiser, it began to grow.

Of course then they knew, or thought they knew, it was a seed-baby. But never could they find in the Brazil nut any sign of the little plant, as they had found it in the other seeds.

"I think," said Jack, one day, "that it is not a seed-baby at all, for it hasn't told us anything."

"Humph!" said the Brazil nut.

"You had better keep still, Jack; it will begin to tell you, you don't understand," said Ko, warningly.

"Well," said the Brazil nut, "I might tell you that and tell the truth, but it would be too much trouble. I prefer to talk about myself.

"I grow in the forests of Brazil, where it is the hottest summer all the year round, and I grow on a *very* tall and *very* handsome tree.

"Twenty or thirty of us grow together in a cup that looks something like a cocoanut. We fill the space so full, and are so nicely fitted together, that if any one unpacks us, he can never put us all back again.

"Some of my cousins have lids to their cups, and these lids fall open when the cups get ripe, and drop from the tree, and let the nuts fall out.

"These are called monkey-cups, because the monkeys that live in the forest where we grow like to play with them.

"My cup has no lid, however, but is apt to break in its fall from the tall tree, or else we have to lie and wait and wait for that hard cup to get soft in the wet ground.

"We can swell, I tell you! When we get ready to grow, our shell is not so very hard, for it has soaked until it is rather soft, and we just press against it and burst it open."

"There!" said Ko, "I believe that is the way the hazel nut does it."

"Hazel nut? I don't know any-thing about hazel nut, but that is the way we get out of our shell."

"But where do you keep your ba-by?" asked Jack.

"Keep my baby? Why, you goose, I am *all* baby! I am just a baby — a seed-baby — and nothing else."

"But I can't see your two leaves and your little root, even when I look with papa's glass," said Ko.

"Oh, well! I am not going to tell you *all* my secrets. *I* know how that is, and if you want to, you will have to find out."

"How can we find out?" asked Jack.

"That is your lookout," was the reply; and not another word could that nut be got to say, then or after.

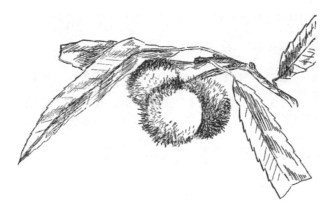

Cradles

"Why *do* you suppose nuts and. things have such dreadful coverings," Jack asked Ko one day, after he had spent" half an hour scrubbing his hands with lemon and salt to get the walnut stains off, so he could go to town with mamma.

The barn floor was covered with butternuts and black walnuts and their "shucks," as the boys called the juicy outer covering.

They had made themselves each a flail such as farmers used to use to thresh out wheat and rye, and had been pounding away for a day or two to get the nuts out of their "shucks."

As threshing is generally done by machinery now, a good many boys and girls have never seen a flail. So I must tell you it is two strong sticks, the longest one as long as your arm, or longer. They are fastened together with a bit of rope or leather. You hold one end, and with the other pound the grain or whatever you wish to loosen from its husk.

Those who have gathered butternuts and black walnuts know what a thick, juicy hull the nuts are covered with, and how the juice from these hulls has a very bad taste and stains the fingers a deep, rich brown, which stays a long time.

It is very hard to remove even if one tries. Boys usually do not try, — they let it wear off.

Jack and Ko generally did not trouble themselves much about it, but this time Jack had an invitation to go to the city with his mother to a birthday dinner with half a dozen cousins about his own age. That is, he could go if he could get his hands clean.

He knew there would be fun, — games, and stories, and *plenty* of ice cream. So he was doing his best with a lemon and a saucer of salt, and Ko was helping him.

"I think," said Ko, "that I know why nuts are covered up this way. Ever since the almond scolded so when I said it was hard because it had to fall a good way, I've been thinking about it."

So you see it sometimes does children good to scold them.

"Well, out with it!" said Jack, who was much more interested just then in getting his hands clean than in hearing about nuts.

"Don't you remember," said Ko, "the almonds Uncle John sent us from California? those fresh ones? They had an outside covering a little like the butternuts, only not so much so. Well, you remember what the Madeira nut said about not coming out of its shell? It was so sweet it might get eaten. Now I believe that's why nuts have such a mean shuck."

"But hickory nuts don't, nor chestnuts," said Jack. "You pick them up as clean and shiny as you please. Ow!" he roared in the same breath, "don't rub *all* the skin off my fingers!"

"I guess that hand is about as clean as I can get it, and leave any skin on," said Ko, surveying the very red little paw which he had been scrubbing. "I think brown hands look about as well as red ones, but mother doesn't seem to."

"I should say hickory nuts *do* have bad-tasting shucks, until they get ripe and fall out," he went on, seizing Jack's other hand, and vigorously applying lemon and salt to the finger ends.

"Sometimes the shucks get dry and let the ripe nuts out, and sometimes they stay on the nuts and fall off with them."

"That's about it," said a walnut that had rolled across the barn floor, near where they were sitting. "You see our shells are quite soft at first, and our seeds, though not as sweet as when we are ripe, are still pretty good to eat. So we just cover the whole thing over with the bitterest, stingingest rind we can manage to make, and keep it until we are too hard for birds and most insects. Even then, we walnuts keep our hulls, but hickory nuts drop out of theirs,. and so do chestnuts."

"Chestnut burrs don't need to taste *very* bad," said Jack, laughing. "Nothing would want to bite one again after it had once got a few stickers in its mouth."

"No indeed," said Ko; "come to think of it, *all* nuts have some sort of horrid outside to them. Remember how sour the hazel burr is?"

"The Madeira nut doesn't," said Jack.

"You can't say that," said Ko, "for you don't know how it grows. I shouldn't wonder if it has, for it is ever so much like a hickory nut."

"Well, Brazil nuts," persisted Jack.

"Goodness, boy! Don't you remember what they told you about the hard cups they grow in? That's for the same thing, only it is hard instead of tasting nasty."

"It's just this way," said the walnut, from its place in the corner. "All of us nuts have to be taken care of while we are growing. Now what do you keep your babies in?"

"In their mothers' arms," said Jack.

"I mean when they're asleep," said the nut.

"Cradles," answered Jack. "Well, that's the way with us. These bad-tasting or hard husks are just the cradles to keep our babies safe until they are strong enough to help themselves a little."

"Goodness!" said Jack.

"Yes," said the walnut, "that's the way it is."

"I believe all seeds have cradles, come to think of it," said Ko; "for the beans have their tough pods, and the peas, too. Even the pigs won't eat bean-pods."

"How about apples?" demanded Jack.

"They taste bad until they 're 'most ripe," said Ko; "but then it seems just as if they asked to be eaten."

"Yes, — and cherries, and peaches, and plums, and oh, lots of things!" added Jack.

"I can tell you about that," said the walnut, proud of being able to tell the boys so many things. "You see, almonds and plums are very much alike, only almonds have big, sweet seeds and not very hard shells. Now, they have bad-tasting husks to keep the seeds from being eaten. Well, plums have bitter seeds and very hard shells, so they have sweet and juicy hulls, which birds and people like to eat. But they throw away the seed, which may chance to fall in a place where it can grow. So with apples and pears, — the core is tough and keeps the seeds from being eaten.

"It is a good thing for the seeds to be carried away from the tree where they grow and thrown in a place where there is more room for them to live."

"There! don't you think that is done?" Jack demanded, pulling his hand away from Ko, and looking at it.

"Yes, I guess you'll do now," was the reply. "If they ask whether we took you for a lobster and tried to boil you, tell them it's scrubbing and not boiling that's made you so red."

"Good-by, Ko," said Jack; "I'll eat an extra plate of ice cream for you."

But Ko did not look very grateful for Jack's generous offer.

"I wish they'd invited me, too," he said.

"Oh, it's Tom's birthday soon, and he's your size, you know, and it will be your turn to go; then I'll have to stay home and think about it," said Jack, consolingly.

And off he went.

Apple Seeds

"Give me one!" demanded Jack, a few days later, as he found his brother disposing of a big apple.

"This is all I have, but I'll give you a bite," Ko replied.

"Why can't you give me half?" persisted Jack, who grew hungrier and hungrier for that apple, as he saw his chances of having it diminish.

"Well, piggy-wig, I will."

So Ko cut the apple in two, and in doing so, cut across the core, of course.

"My!" said Jack, who had come to look much more closely at things since the seeds began to talk to him. "What a cunning cradle those little black babies have!" They *are* babies, aren't they, Ko, — those apple seeds'?"

"Of course," said Ko, with a very superior air.

"How do you know?" rang out the apple seed's voice, like a little silver bell.

"I don't — exactly," said Ko, good-naturedly, "I just *guessed* so, because so many seeds are just the plants' babies, and then the walnut said something about it, though I don't remember just what."

"There, there, never mind looking!" pealed out the silver voice again, as Ko took up the seed to examine it.

"How am I going to find out?" demanded Ko.

"Oh, plant me! I would like that so much better than being pulled to pieces. And you would learn just as much — and more."

"All right," and Ko tucked the apple seed under the ground in the corner of his garden.

Well, it *was* a baby, for in the spring it started to grow, and Ko let it alone, and after a few years, — what do you think? He picked golden apples from that little black apple seed's tree!

"I say," said Jack, watching Ko plant it, "what a scheme it would be to plant all the apple seeds, and peach seeds, and pear seeds, and plum seeds, — and everything. Just plant a seed wherever there's a spot big enough for a tree."

"I heard about a man who did that," said Ko. "He planted something whenever he went for a walk. He put fruit trees in the fields and on the edge of the woods. Wherever he went the fruit trees grew. People found fruit in unexpected places, and were glad. Even when he had been dead a great many years, the people picked his fruit."

"That is nice," said Jack. "I mean to save my seeds."

"It puzzles me about plums and things," said Ko. "Let 's ask mother for some plums and peaches, and see how they manage about their seeds. I guess the stones *are* seeds, and that they split open to let the baby out."

Perhaps you think I am going to tell you all that Jack and Ko found out about  the pits of things, — but you are *very* much mistaken. If you want to know these things, as far as I am concerned, you will have to go to work and find them out for your-selves. And it isn't a hard matter, either; anybody with a pair of eyes and any sort of a mind can do it pretty well.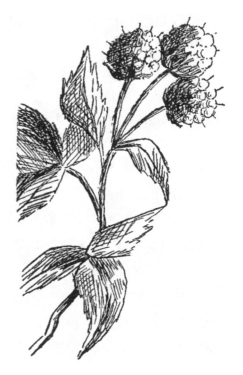

But this I will tell you, — that Jack and Ko did not stop asking and looking, and when the next summer came, and they could pick the little seeds from the out-side of the strawberries, and blackberries, and raspber-ries, and from the inside of the blueberries, and gooseberries, and currants, and grapes, and found these mites of seeds to be just tiny strawberry, and raspberry, and blackberry, and currant, and gooseberry babies, they thought they knew some-thing about seeds!

They gathered grain, too, that summer, — heads of wheat, and barley, and oats, and ears of corn; and they found them filled with grains, and they said these of grains were seeds, and that each seed was a baby. They ended by saying that every seed — even the dandelion, and thistledown, and the tiniest poppy or turnip seed — was a baby, and nothing but a baby. And maybe they were right about that.

But they did more than this, — what do you think? They said that *everything* had to grow from a seed, and that there was no other way to manage it — which shows how very, very little they knew after all.

For it is one thing to say that a lily can grow from a seed, but quite another thing to say it cannot grow *except* from a seed.

And right there is where they made their mistake.

Sweet Kittie Clover

It was sweet Kittie Clover who found that lilies, and berry bushes, and some other things grow by bulbs and buds instead of by seeds.

You all know Kittie; at least, everybody used to know her, for there was a song about her, beginning, "Sweet Kittie Clover, she bothers me so."

Well, it was Kittie who showed Jack and Ko the funny little black bulbs in the armpits — no, the leaf-pits — of the big tiger-lily, and how the sprouts that made new bushes sometimes came out of the roots of the old bushes, instead of out of seeds.

But she agreed with the boys that a great many things in the plant world had to start from seeds.

She used to gather the flower seeds and soak them until they had become soft, and then with her father's big magnifying glass, she would look at the little plants curled up in the seeds.

"Come over here and see something," she called to Jack and Ko one morning, for they were next-door neighbors.

Kittie was about half way between Jack and Ko in age, and the three played together a great deal of the time. Of course the boys had told her all the things the plants had said to them. This had pleased her so much that she, too, began talking to the flowers and other live things about her.

She used to get into mischief very often and bother people, and I suppose that is what the song meant.

To-day she had to stay in the house, because she had "accidentally, on purpose," as the boys said, walked through a puddle of water and got her feet soaking wet.

So there she sat, wishing for something to do, when she caught sight of the morning-glory vines, and all at once she remembered she had put some seeds to soak the day before. This was just the time to look at them, so she ran and got them.

Then she called the boys, for she thought she really had something worth showing.

Jack and Ko came racing over at Kittie's call, glad of an excuse to see her, for they always felt badly when she was in disgrace, almost as badly as if they had been the cause of it.

Sometimes they were the cause of it, and helped her get into mischief, but they were always sorry — when it was too late!

It is so very easy to get into mischief! Kittie said she never had to try a bit. She had to try hard to do every-thing else, but that seemed to do itself.

The boys were glad to see Kittie and glad to see what she had to show them.

Everybody remembers how the morning-glory looks when it first comes out of the ground. Two blunt little leaves appear that do not look at all like the heart-shaped ones that come later.

Well, Kittie slipped off the black skin of the seed, and inside she found, packed about by some clear, jelly-like material, these same two little leaves, as blunt as you please, and all curled up in the seed.

"That's worth seeing!" said Ko. "It has its food separate from its cotyledons."

"Is that jelly its food?" demanded Jack.

"It must be," said Ko. And Kittie thought so, too.

After a while the morning-glory told them all about it, and Ko was quite proud to learn he had guessed right. The jelly *is* the food, the morning-glory said.

Then Kittle soaked a lot of four-o'clock seeds, and in each of them found the tender little plant, with no starch to speak of stored in its cotyledons, but instead, lying embedded in a floury mass of food.

It would take a long time to tell of all the queer and lovely seed-babies Kittie and the boys saw in the flowers that summer. They looked at wild flowers as well as at those in the garden, and everywhere the story was the same. In the seed was stored away the plant-baby.

They had a lot of fun doing it, and anybody who likes can have just as much fun, for the seeds are always ready to show their treasures.

A New Kind of Seed

One day Kittie came upon something funny enough!

She found what she took to be a lot of round white seeds growing on the back of a leaf.

"I didn't know seeds grew that way," Jack said, shaking his head over them. "Let's soak them," said he. So they soaked a few, but when they opened them they could find no seed-baby, only something soft and without any form at all.

How Ko laughed when he found what they were doing!

"You precious — pair — of — ninnies!" he roared.

"Well, what ails you?" demanded Jack, indignantly.

"Oh, my goodness! soaking — eggs — to make them grow!" gasped Ko.

"Eggs, nothing of the sort!" retorted Jack.

But Ko was right, as time proved; for one day, out of these little seeds, as Jack and Kittie persisted in calling them, there came creeping the very funniest and tiniest of caterpillars.

"I told you so," said Ko.

"Seeds and eggs are the same thing, anyway," said Jack, coolly.

"Yes," Kittie hastened to add, "the very same thing, only little plants hatch out of seeds, and little animals out of eggs."

"There may be something in that," Ko admitted.

"You a seed-baby?" Jack demanded, very gently poking one of the little caterpillars that had already gone to work to eat the edge off the apple leaf upon which it had been hatched.

But if it was a seed-baby, it did not say so. It just rolled up into a ball and fell off the leaf on the ground.

"You've lost it!" screamed Kittie.

"It lost itself," protested Jack, "and anyway, I guess that kind of a seed-baby can take care of itself even if it is lost. They don't seem to have to be very old to do that."

The children were so. anxious to keep their little caterpillars, that Kittie' s mother gave them a piece of netting, which they tied over the branch where' the caterpillars were, and so all summer the two boys and Kittie watched them grow.

Only Kittie's father said they must be sure that none of them escaped, for he didn't want his whole orchard eaten up by them.

"How they *do* eat," said Ko, as he removed them for the third time to fresh branches, because there were no leaves left on the old ones.

"Their skins are falling off!" Jack exclaimed, one day. And sure enough, it was true. They crawled out of their skins plumper and bigger than they were before.

"They got too big for their skins," said Kittie.

"It's a handy way to grow," Jack said. "You just fill up your old skin, then pop it open and creep out with a brand new and bigger one on you."

When they had changed their skins a number of times, and grown many times as large as they were at first, all the caterpillars spun soft cocoons and closed the doors behind them.

When winter came Kittie carried these little cocoons into the house, and towards spring out came, not the caterpillars, but in their place bright little millers.

"I must say," Jack remarked, "those *were* queer seeds you found, Kittie."

"And I must say," added Kittie, "that the butterflies take a roundabout way to get here."

"They 're not butterflies," said Jack, "they 're millers."

"It's about the same thing, smarty," Kittie retorted.

Bumble-Bees

If anybody were to suppose that Kittie and Ko and Jack were satisfied with caterpillars' eggs that summer, "right dar's whar he broke his merlasses jug," as Uncle Remus would say. For they took to hunting eggs just as they had been hunting seeds before, and if they didn't find as many eggs as they did seeds, at least they found a good many.

And although they could not find the baby caterpillars, and ants, and flies, and bugs in the eggs when they broke them open, if they watched them long enough with- out breaking, the little  creatures were sure to grow and hatch out of them soon- er or later.

"*Everything* lays eggs, I believe," Jack said, one day.

"Do you suppose bumble-bees do? "asked Kittie, — then added very mysteriously, "I know where there's a bumblebee's nest."

"How do you know it's a nest?" demanded Ko.

"Oh, because," said Kittie.

"Humph!" said Jack, "that's no reason."

"Well, I know it is, and if you want to get it, I'll show you where to find it," said Kittie.

"Come along then," said Ko.

So they went with her to a place in the corner of the or-chard where an old plank was lying in the grass.

"There, it's under that," she said, pointing to the plank.

The boys looked, and presently a big bumble-bee came blundering out from a hole at the edge of the plank.

"Well, I believe it's so," said Ko, — then added, "Now you had better run, Kittie, for I 'm going to lift up that plank."

"You don't dare," said Kittie.

"You'll see if I don't," he replied, proudly; "now run, or you'll get stung."

"Who's afraid?" demanded Kittie, standing her ground. "I'm not going to run."

"You'll get stung," said Jack, warningly.

"So will you," retorted Kittie.

"Oh, boys don't mind such things," said Ko, with a very fine air.

"Neither do girls," replied Kittie, obstinately.

"Well, get stung if you want to!" and Ko suddenly seized one end of the plank and raised it a little. It was too heavy for him to move much, but the little he did stir it, sent out a swarm of very lively and *very* angry bumblebees.

"There's one on your apron, Kittie!" yelled Jack, dancing around and fighting a bee that seemed determined to make his acquaintance.

"I know it," Kittie screamed back, trying hard not to cry and putting her hands behind her, while the bee came buzzing up her apron. But for some reason it tumbled off and she was saved.

Just then Ko darted past her, making some very queer noises as he went.

"Boys don't mind such things," naughty Kittie called out, running after him.

And then Jack passed her, bawling as if he were being killed.

"Boys don't" — Kittie began, but just then something struck her on the cheek, and she nearly fell over, it hurt so, and then something equally dreadful happened to the back of her neck, and she followed Ko and Jack, bawling as loudly as they.

Kittie's mother put something on all the stings to take out the pain, and then got a book about bees and showed the children pictures of how they make their nests, and showed them a picture of the dainty little rooms where the eggs are stored away.

"It's just a bee cradle," said Jack, studying one carefully.

"Yes, that's it," said Ko. "I wish we could have seen them," said Kittie, wistfully. "It was mean of the bees not to let us."

"They were afraid you would spoil their nest and kill their young ones," mother replied. "You can hardly blame them for defending themselves.

"Suppose some great giant came to tear our house down, and carry off baby Belle to look at her under a microscope, what would you feel like doing?"

"I'd chop his head off," said Jack, promptly.

"That's the way the bees felt about it," said mother.

"Only they couldn't chop our heads off, so they stung them off," said Kittie, solemnly, caressing the great lump on her cheek.

"I hope you've got cheek enough, Kittie," said Ko, tormentingly.

"Well, my eye isn't swelled shut, anyway," she replied, looking straight at the spot where Ko's merry brown eye had gone into eclipse. "I know one thing," she added, "boys make as much fuss as girls, after all."

"And girls hate to get stung as much as boys do," added Jack.

"I know another thing," put in Ko. "I *think* I'm acquainted with a boy who won't look for bumble-bees' eggs again until he learns a better way to do it."

Frogs

Such lots of queer eggs as Kittie and Ko and Jack found that summer and the next! Once started looking for eggs they found them everywhere. Even in the winter they found spi-ders' eggs in the cellar, and the boys' father told the children about  the grasshoppers' eggs lying in the ground where the mother grasshopper had laid them, all ready to hatch into little grasshoppers when the spring came.

"We'll be on hand when spring comes," Jack said; and sure enough they were, and about the first thing they found were the frogs' eggs in the ponds.

These eggs were little round balls about as big as peas, dark-colored on one side, and a dozen or more encased in something that looked like colorless jelly.

The children put some of these egg masses in a jar of water and watched them. After a while they hatched into tadpoles, or pollywogs, as the children called them.

I wonder why things don't hatch right out, instead of hatching into something else first," Kittie said, as she looked at them.

"I wonder, too," said Jack. "Butterflies' eggs make caterpillars, flies' eggs make maggots, beetles' eggs make grubs, frogs' eggs make pollywogs, — and after a while the caterpillars turn into butterflies, and the maggots into flies, and the grubs into beetles, and the pollywogs into frogs. It's an awful topsy-turvy sort of do."

"But they all come out right in the end," said Kittie.

"I'm going to keep my eye on these fellows," said Jack, looking into the jar of pollywogs, "and see them get their legs."

"There's one already got hind legs," said Kittie, pointing to a black little pollywog, and sure enough he was the proud possessor of two very tiny legs.

It was not long before they all had hind legs, and a right merry time they had swimming about with their stout little tails, with their new legs to help them.

"I believe their front legs come out of these little pockets where the gills are," Jack said, one day. "It seems to me I can see them in there."

"I believe you're right," said Ko.

And he was; for one day, out of those very same openings there slipped the little forelegs.

"I tell you, they're getting a new mouth," Kittie declared, one day. The boys laughed at this, but they laughed too soon, for the pollywogs *were* getting new mouths.

Their old mouths, which were just little round openings, by means of which they greedily ate the breadcrumbs and bits of meat the children fed them, disappeared, and fine, wide frog mouths opened in another place. Nose openings appeared too, and finally the tails began to shrink. It was not long after this that the pollywogs lost their tails entirely. They just shrank and shrank until no tails were left, and in short, the brown pollywogs turned into little green frogs.

"One of them's dead! The biggest one, too!" cried Kittie, one morning.

Sure enough, the little thing was lying on its back in the water.

"I think it is drowned," said Mother, coming at Kittie's cries to see what had happened.

"Drowned!" exclaimed all three children, for the boys always came over the first thing after breakfast to look at the "pollys," as they called their pets.

"Yes," said Mother, "it seems strange at first, but you must remember that frogs have lungs like ours, and breathe air. They go under water and sometimes stay a good while, but after all, only as long as they can hold their breath. When they want to breathe they have to come to the top.

"Now these little fellows, as long as they are pollywogs, breathe with gills, like fishes; but when they turn into frogs they lose their gills and get lungs. This water is very deep for them; and this one, which has turned wholly into a frog, was not able to stay on top long enough to get all the air it needed.

"You will have to put them in a shallower dish, and put in some stones, so they can come out when they get ready."

"Poor little thing," said Kittie, laying the froggie on its back on her hand. "I'm going to try 'monia, — that brings people to, sometimes, and maybe it's only in a faint."

So she got the ammonia bottle and held it to the froggie's nose. Well, what do you think happened?

Froggie's leg jerked! Kittie was so excited that she spilled a drop of ammonia on one little foot. This made froggie jump in earnest, and pretty soon he was sitting up, "winking" his throat, as Jack said, just like any grown-up frog.

He soon recovered from his drowning, but the ammonia had hurt the tender little foot so that it never grew quite right, and when he had grown to be a big fellow, and ate as many flies and other insects as the children could get for him, he always had one "game leg," as Ko said, in memory of the time when he was nearly drowned.

This is a true story, every word of it, and if you want to have some fun, my wise little readers, I advise you to get some frogs' eggs next spring for yourself. You can watch the legs come out, and the nose and mouth appear.

Only be careful and not drown your froggies when they get through being tadpoles, and be sure to feed them. And be *very* sure to keep them in plenty of fresh water from the start, — otherwise they will die.

Other Eggs

When you once begin to look for things you can always find them. Kittie and the boys saw many eggs that spring besides frogs' eggs.

They found a lot of turtles' eggs, for one thing, and even some snakes' eggs.

And the good old sun hatched these eggs with his warm rays, just as well as if he had been their mother.

The turtles and snakes did not hatch their own eggs. My, no! They left that for the sun to do. They did lay them in the warm sand, though, where the sun could get to them; and there the children found them and left them, and went very often to see them. But do you think they saw the little turtles and snakes? Not a bit of it.

They forgot all about them for a few days, and when they went to look they found it was all over with, and only a lot of empty shells left. They nearly cried, they were so disappointed. Every little turtle and every little snake had gone off about its business, and they could not find one, though they searched a long time.

They found fishes' eggs, too, under the stones in a little stream that ran through a meadow near the house, and these they really did watch hatch into little fishes. For Ko built a wall of stones about the place where the eggs were, loose enough to let the water run in and out, but tight enough to prevent the little fishes from getting away.

That summer, too, the boys and their parents went to the seashore to stay three weeks and took Kittie with them.

There was wading, and bathing, and swimming, and sailing, and in the course of their wadings and sailings the children found many curious things.

What pleased them as well as anything, they found the eggs of many strange creatures.

They found that starfish and sea-urchins lay eggs. But what surprised them most of all, — they learned that "seashells" lay eggs! At least, the animals that live in the shells do.

And such queer cradles as some of these eggs had!

Those of the conch shell were long lines of flat cases like pods. Jack said; and in these pods were the tiniest little conch shells, so very little that they had to look through the magnifying glass to *really* see them.

SHARK'S EGGS.

And the sharks' eggs! Safe in their tough black cradles with long tendrils at the four corners, they lay. The tendrils, they were told, fastened the sharks' eggs to the weeds and things in the bottom of the sea, so they wouldn't be dashed about by the waves, and the baby sharks could have a chance to grow in safety.

61

"I don't see why such ugly things as sharks, that sometimes eat people up, need have their eggs so well cared for," Kittie said, one day.

"*Everything's* eggs are cared for," Jack said, "and I believe almost everything lays eggs, too."

"Everything that's alive has to come out of an egg or a seed, I believe," said Ko.

And he wasn't so very far wrong!

Birds' Eggs

Of course with all their egg and seed hunting the children did not forget the birds.

They had chickens and pigeons to watch, and there were all the wild birds to build nests for them.

A great many birds built in their yards, because the birds seemed to know they would be safe there.

Of course the children often went and looked into the nests where they were low enough so they could. But they were careful about it, and never handled the eggs or the young birds. The old birds seemed to know they had just come to visit, and treated them quite politely.

The catbird that had its nest in the lilac bush, though, was sometimes rather cross, and would fly at them and scream.

"I must reason with that catbird," Kittie said.

So she sat down and reasoned with it, and the children thought it behaved rather better after that. For myself, I have no doubt it did.

"Oh, mommy, mommy, de nest is full of little kitten-birds!" baby Belle called out, one day. She was getting to be very much of a talker, and was also very much interested in watching the birds and things with the other children.

Sister Kittie ran to look, and sure enough there were three little dots of catbirds.

The man who took care of the garden had lifted baby Belle up so she could see them.

"I wonder what is in it," Jack said that same day, as he held a little box in his hand that the postman had brought. It had his name on it, and he felt proud, I can tell you.

"Why don't you open it?" demanded Ko.

"You go call Kittie and I will," he said.

So Ko got Kittie to come, and then Jack opened the box.

It was from Uncle John, who was then in Florida. He had heard about the boys' interest in looking for eggs, and had sent them — guess what?

A long, white alligator's egg.

"Think of an alligator coming out of a little thing like that!" said Kittie.

"No worse than that old rooster coming out of a little hen's egg," said Ko, firing a chip at the rooster, who merely flapped his wings and crowed in reply.

"But an alligator is as b-i-g as a big man, and ever so much bigger," Kittie objected.

"Not when it is hatched," persisted Ko.

"No, and then it's all so queer about eggs, anyway," admitted Kittie; "they *do* hatch out such queer things."

"I wonder if angle worms come out of eggs, too," Jack said, as a robin hopped across the path with a fine fat angle worm in his bill.

"No doubt of it," said Ko.

And to be sure there was no doubt of it, he went and asked his father, who told him some very interesting things about angle worms' eggs.

But I am not going to tell you what it was, for there are a *few* things I should like to leave for you to find out for yourselves.

Only this I will say, — if you look in the right place, at the right time, you no doubt will be able to find any quantity of angle worms' eggs.

And you can watch them hatch out, too, if you know how to go about it.

Perhaps the angle worms will tell you how that is. But I am not going to.

"I have told you enough," as the bean said to Jack.

And like Jack, I hope you will say, "Well, I guess I can find out some more for myself."

For so you can. If you keep your eyes open and look at things, there is no end to what you will find.

The more you look, the more you will want to, — that's the best of it.

Anybody can make beans and other things talk, and I think it is rather a shame for people not to know about beans.

Don't you?

CPSIA information can be obtained
at www.ICGtesting.com
Printed in the USA
BVHW071432270820
587359BV00002B/110